Animal Spirits

paintings by *Susan Seddon Boulet*

2001 DELUXE ENGAGEMENT BOOK

Catalog No. 201008
Published by Pomegranate Communications, Inc.
© 2000 The Susan Eleanor Boulet Trust
ISBN 0-7649-1136-8

Available in the U.S. and Canada from Pomegranate Communications, Inc.,
Box 6099, Rohnert Park, California 94927
Available in the U.K. and mainland Europe from Pomegranate Europe Ltd.,
Fullbridge House, Fullbridge, Maldon, Essex CM9 4LE, England
Available in Australia from Boobook Publications Pty. Ltd.,
P.O. Box 163 or Freepost 1, Tea Gardens, NSW 2324
Available in New Zealand from Randy Horwood Ltd., P.O. Box 32-077, Devonport, Auckland
Available in Asia (including the Middle East), Africa, and Latin America from
Pomegranate International Sales, 113 Babcombe Drive, Thornhill, Ontario L3T 1M9, Canada

Pomegranate publishes more of Susan Seddon Boulet's paintings in the 2001 calendars *Unicorns*, *Shaman*, *Goddesses*, and *Signs of the Zodiac*. Her work is also available in notecards, holiday cards, postcards, books of postcards, posters, bookmarks, a deck of Knowledge Cards™, and art magnets, as well as in the books *Buffalo Gals, Won't You Come Out Tonight*; *Susan Seddon Boulet: The Goddess Paintings*; *Shaman: the Paintings of Susan Seddon Boulet*; *The Power of the Bear: Paintings by Susan Seddon Boulet*; and *Susan Seddon Boulet: A Retrospective*.

Our products and publications include books, posters, postcards and books of postcards, notecards and boxed notecard sets, magnets, mousepads, Knowledge Cards™, appointment books and journals, screensavers, and bookmarks. For more information or to place an order, please contact Pomegranate Communications, Inc.: 1-800-227-1428; www.pomegranate.com.

Front cover: *Untitled*, 1975 (detail)
Designed by Shannon Lemme
Printed in Korea

All astronomical data supplied in this calendar are expressed in Greenwich Mean Time (GMT).
American, Canadian, and U.K. holidays and moon phases are noted.

● NEW MOON   ◗ FIRST QUARTER   ○ FULL MOON   ◖ LAST QUARTER

From the earliest times, humans have recognized and venerated the special kinship they have with the beasts. In Native American traditions, for example, animals are the messengers of the Great Spirit and every individual has a personal animal totem ("totem" derives from the Algonquian *nto'tem*, meaning "my kin"). Communicating through dreams and visions, animals offer the power of healing, provide comfort in times of trouble, and serve as guides to a greater self-awareness.

Susan Seddon Boulet (1941–1997) had a special relationship with animals, and she understood their power. As a child growing up on a Brazilian farm she developed a deep affection for all beasts and loved making colorful sketches of them. Later in her career, Boulet was deeply inspired by the stories of animal spirits found in ancient myths and shamanic traditions; her paintings brought these legends to life, offering glimpses of an ethereal world that exists beyond the horizons of ordinary reality. Renowned for finely detailed and complex imagery, Boulet's paintings draw viewers into an enchanted realm that resonates with unspoken, universal truths.

Bast, 1978

Untitled, 1976

monday
1 1

NEW YEAR'S DAY

tuesday
)) **2** 2

BANK HOLIDAY (SCOTLAND)

wednesday
3 3

thursday
4 4

TERA - R. UPPER THORACIC
JARED - L. FEMUR - R. L2
DYLLON - R. FEMUR - REFLEXOLOGY

friday
5 5

Lion

The Self is often symbolized as an animal, representing our instinctive nature and its connectedness with one's surroundings. . . . This relation of the Self to all surrounding nature and even the cosmos comes from the fact that the "nuclear atom" of our psyche is somehow woven into the whole world, both outer and inner.

—Carl Jung

GLORIA - L 5 LEFT.
BACH REMEDY

saturday
6 6

sunday
7 7

JAROD - REFLEXOLOGY

M	T	W	T	F	S	S	M	T	W	T	F	S	S	M	T	W	T	F	S	S	M	T	W	T	F	S	S	M	T	W
1	2	3	4	5	6	7	8	9	10	11	12	13	14	15	16	17	18	19	20	21	22	23	24	25	26	27	28	29	30	31

January

JANUARY

monday
8

tuesday
9

wednesday
10

thursday
11
DYLLON - LEFT HEEL

friday
12
DYLLON - REFLEXOLOGY
- C-4
- LOWER THORASIC RIGHT

saturday
13
DYLLON - THORASIC - UPPER
- LOWER - RIGHT

sunday
14

notes

monday
19
15

MARTIN LUTHER KING JR. DAY

✳ HINTON ALBERTA **tuesday**
☾ ## 16
16

DORIS HOPE   9:00 AM
DOUG BLOCHA   11:00
PARLISE LASONDER 1:30

wednesday
17
17

DEB CORLESS   11:00 AM
BEV BLOCHA   5:00 PM
SYLVIA METCALF   1:30 PM
DORIS HOPE   7:00 PM

thursday
18
18

ROCKY N.   9:00
LENI   11:00
ANNE HAMM   1:30
ELI LASONDER   3:30
SAMUEL LASONDER   4:30
LEANNE SCOTT   7:00

friday
19
19

saturday
20
20

Night Form, 1973

JAN 3:00PM CHILLIWACK
SHIRLEY BARBER 7:00 PM

sunday
21
21

M T W T F S S M T W T F S S M T W T F S S M T W T F S S M T W
1 2 3 4 5 6 7 8 9 10 11 12 13 14 15 16 17 18 19 20 21 22 23 24 25 26 27 28 29 30 31

January

Brother Dove, 1975

monday
22
22

Bunny Anderson 1:30
Shirley Reid 2:30
Sean Lervold 3:30 PM.
Herb Brokop 6:30

tuesday
23
23

Vac Scott 4:00 PM
Tom Scott 5:00 PM

Liz Smith 2:30 PM

wednesday
● 24
24

Barb Gandy 10:30 AM
604-931-6640 - Ca. 306-8057

thursday
25
25

friday
26
26

Dove

What is man without the beasts? If all the
beasts were gone, men would die from a
great loneliness of spirit. For whatever
happens to the beasts soon happens to
the man. All things are connected.
—Chief Seattle

saturday
27
27

sunday
28
28

M	T	W	T	F	S	S	M	T	W	T	F	S	S	M	T	W	T	F	S	S	M	T	W	T	F	S	S	M	T	W
1	2	3	4	5	6	7	8	9	10	11	12	13	14	15	16	17	18	19	20	21	22	23	24	25	26	27	28	29	30	31

January

monday
29 **29** _____

tuesday
30 **30** _____

wednesday
31 **31**   DYLLON : 6:30

thursday
32 **1**   D

friday
33 **2** _____

saturday
34 **3**   DYLLON   7:30 P.M. — REFLEXOLOGY

sunday
35 **4**   _____   *notes* _____

monday
5 36

GAYLE K.   3:00 PM

tuesday
6 37

wednesday
7 38

(RMT) - PETER GRAINGER 3:30 PM
        - C 5 & 6 ON LEFT.

GLORIA -   4:30 PM

thursday
○ 8 39

GEORGE ANNALA
    1:00 PM

friday
9 40

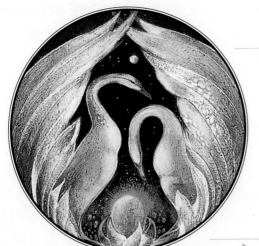

saturday
10 41

GEORGE ANNALA
    3:30 PM

sunday
11 42

Untitled, 1980

DYLLON - RIGHT HIP - LOWER THORASIC.
VERA -

T F S S M T W T F S S M T W T F S S M T W T F S S M T W
1 2 3 4 5 6 7 8 9 10 11 12 13 14 15 16 17 18 19 20 21 22 23 24 25 26 27 28
February

Woodland Tales, 1975

LINCOLN'S BIRTHDAY

GAYLE K.   3:00 PM

monday
12 43

GLORIA - L2 ON LEFT
- BACH REMEDY

tuesday
13 44

VALENTINE'S DAY

wednesday
14 45

Deer

When the rising sun looks,
Walk out, they tell me.
When I went there, she who walks on
   the water was wild,
Her walk was wild, her eye was wild,
I came as she brought me some.

With a bone medicine belt not wild,
   I came to her.
With wind's footprints not wild,
   I came near her.
With a yellow spotted belt not wild,
   I came near her.
With a bone medicine shirt not wild,
   I came near her.
      —Song of the Deer Ceremony,
        San Carlos Apache

DONU STARR   12:30 PM
832-5480

thursday
15 46

JARED - REFLEXOLOGY
7:30 PM

friday
16 47

DYLLON - NECK
- REFLEXOLOGY
7:30 PM

saturday
17 48

SUSAN WRIGHT   10:00 AM
832-8119
GIFT CERT.

sunday
18 49

T F S S M T W T F S S M T W T F S S M T W T F S S M T W
1 2 3 4 5 6 7 8 9 10 11 12 13 14 15 16 17 18 19 20 21 22 23 24 25 26 27 28

February

FEBRUARY

monday
50 **19**   BONNIE   11:00 AM   PRESIDENTS' DAY

tuesday
51 **20**

wednesday
52 **21**

thursday
53 **22**   WASHINGTON'S BIRTHDAY

friday
54 **23** ●

saturday
55 **24**

sunday   *notes*
56 **25**

monday
26 57

GAIL KURTA 3:00 PM 832-0425
TRACY MUNDY 1:00 PM 833-0102

tuesday
27 58

wednesday
28 59

ASH WEDNESDAY

thursday
1 60

VIOLA : 11:00 AM
675-2749
(FRIEND OF GLORIAS)

friday
2 61

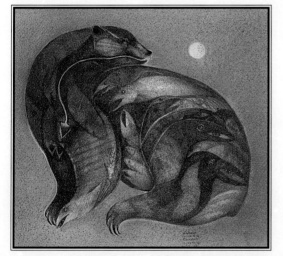

saturday
☽ **3** 62

sunday
4 63

Bear Totem

T	F	S	S	M	T	W	T	F	S	S	M	T	W	T	F	S	S	M	T	W	T	F	S	S	M	T	W	T	F	S
1	2	3	4	5	6	7	8	9	10	11	12	13	14	15	16	17	18	19	20	21	22	23	24	25	26	27	28	29	30	31

March

Moon Shield, 1995

_____ monday
5 64

_____ tuesday
6 65

_____ wednesday
7 66

_____ thursday
8 67

DAVE COWAN   11:00 AM
OFFICE 804-0199
HM 804-0802

Jaguar

I think I could turn and live with animals, they are so placid
   and self-contain'd,
I stand and look at them long and long.

_____ friday
○ 9 68

They do not sweat and whine about their condition,
. . . .

Not one is dissatisfied, not one is demented with the mania
   of owning things,

_____ saturday
10 69

Not one kneels to another, nor to his kind that lived
   thousands of years ago,
Not one is respectable or unhappy over the whole earth.
             —Walt Whitman, *Song of Myself, 32*

_____ sunday
11 70

T	F	S	S	M	T	W	T	F	S	S	M	T	W	T	F	S	S	M	T	W	T	F	S	S	M	T	W	T	F	S
1	2	3	4	5	6	7	8	9	10	11	12	13	14	15	16	17	18	19	20	21	22	23	24	25	26	27	28	29	30	31

March

MARCH

monday
71 12

JEFF
RADAR
GLORIA

tuesday
72 13

wednesday
73 14

thursday
74 15

friday
75 16 ☽

⑧

saturday
76 17

ST. PATRICK'S DAY

⑧

sunday
77 18 ————— *notes* —————

⑦

BANK HOLIDAY (N. IRELAND)

APP WITH DAVE COWAN
4:30 P.M. FOR ME

Cottage

(8½)

VERNAL EQUINOX 1:31 P.M. (GMT)

(9½)

(9)

(8)

(8)

(8)

Untitled, 1976

T	F	S	S	M	T	W	T	F	S	S	M	T	W	T	F	S	S	M	T	W	T	F	S	S	M	T	W	T	F	S
1	2	3	4	5	6	7	8	9	10	11	12	13	14	15	16	17	18	19	20	21	22	23	24	25	26	27	28	29	30	31

March

Council of Animals, 1996

monday
26
8
85

tuesday
27
8
86

CONNIE JAMISON

MAGGY — LEFT FOOT

wednesday
28
8
87

thursday
29
8
88

friday
30
8
89

Serpent

But ask now the beasts, and they shall
teach thee; and the fowls of the air,
and they shall tell thee:
Or speak to the earth, and it shall teach
thee; and the fishes of the sea shall
declare unto thee.

—The Book of Job, 12:7–8

GLORIA

saturday
31
8
90

DAYLIGHT SAVING TIME BEGINS

sunday
1
☽
91

S	M	T	W	T	F	S	S	M	T	W	T	F	S	S	M	T	W	T	F	S	S	M	T	W	T	F	S	S	M
1	2	3	4	5	6	7	8	9	10	11	12	13	14	15	16	17	18	19	20	21	22	23	24	25	26	27	28	29	30

April

Sun Spirit, 1975

monday
2 92
(5)

AURO SIMMONSON -11:00 AM
FRENEN LADY.   1:00 PM
MARIE L.

tuesday
3 93
(8)

wednesday
4 94
(8)

thursday
5 95

Horse

In wild flight
I sent the swallows
in wild flight
I made them go
in wild flight
before the clouds were gathered

friday
6 96

In wild flight
I sent my horse
in wild flight
a swallow flying running
in wild flight
before the clouds were gathered

FIRST NIGHT OF PASSOVER

saturday
7 97

—Teton Sioux

PALM SUNDAY

sunday
○ **8** 98

S M T W T F S S M T W T F S S M T W T F S S M T W T F S S M
1 2 3 4 5 6 7 8 9 10 11 12 13 14 15 16 17 18 19 20 21 22 23 24 25 26 27 28 29 30

April

APRIL

monday
99 9

tuesday
100 10

wednesday
101 11
⑦   1:00PM STEVE

thursday
102 12

friday
103 13   GOOD FRIDAY

saturday
104 14

sunday   notes
105 15 ☽   EASTER SUNDAY

monday
16 106

EASTER MONDAY (CANADA, U.K.)

SUE BOLEN
4:00 PM

BRIAN STANOA 10:30
832-2587

MAGGY PYM 3:00
832-4515

tuesday
17 107

wednesday
18 108

thursday
19 109

friday
20 110

Bast, 1978

saturday
21 111

BRENDA B. 2:00PM

sunday
22 112

EARTH DAY GLORIAS 1:45

S M T W T F S S M T W T F S S M T W T F S S M T W T F S S M
1 2 3 4 5 6 7 8 9 10 11 12 13 14 15 16 17 18 19 20 21 22 23 24 25 26 27 28 29 30

April

Cecilia's Dog, 1984

monday ● **23** 113

tuesday 24 114

MAGGY
GLORIA

wednesday 25 115

thursday 26 116

TRADS HOLGA 11:00 TILL 1:00

Dog

give me your dog

my child's gone off

I need a good dog

to find him

friday 27 117

an invisible dog

comes up from somewhere

licks his left hand

and follows

saturday 28 118

     —from a Chukchee (Siberian)
    incantation to bring back the dead

sunday 29 119

S M T W T F S S M T W T F S S M T W T F S S M T W T F S S M
1 2 3 4 5 6 7 8 9 10 11 12 13 14 15 16 17 18 19 20 21 22 23 24 25 26 27 28 29 30

April

monday
120
30 D

MIKE GARROD — 835-4352
10:00 AM

tuesday
121
1

wednesday
122
2

PAT JORGENSON - 675-3827
12:00 PM

thursday
123
3

friday
124
4

AWAY WITH P.O.E. CLASS
TREE PLANTING DRY LAKE

saturday
125
5

CINCO DE MAYO

sunday
126
6

notes

✳ HINTON ALBERTA

monday
7 127

BANK HOLIDAY (U.K.)   MARIE THOMPSON
RONI SIMPSON
DORIS HOPE
SHERRY H
KIM MORROW
DOUG BLOCHA

NORMA MULDUN'S
HORSES - LITTLE HONOUR
= DARLING

tuesday
8 128

SHANE CALLIHOO
FRANCINE
ANNIBELLE
PARISE LASONDER

ELAIN PENNER
FAY McCRACKIN

wednesday
9 129

SHELLEY
CAROL ROSEN
ROCKY N.
DID DEMO VIDEO TAPE AT NIGHT TODAY

thursday
10 130

ALIAN GRIFFITHS
TROY ZIMMER
BEV BLOCHA
BOB CALLIHOO
ELI LASONDER
SAMUEL LASONDER

CLAIRA - NORMA'S MOM

friday
11 131

↑

TRAVEL HOME TODAY
JAROD - DYLLON
TERA - DAD

saturday
12 132

INTRODUCTION DAY
BARRY & YVONNE

WORKED ON 19 PEOPLE   15 MIN SESSIONS

sunday
13 133

MOTHER'S DAY

Untitled, 1973

T	W	T	F	S	S	M	T	W	T	F	S	S	M	T	W	T	F	S	S	M	T	W	T	F	S	S	M	T	W	T
1	2	3	4	5	6	7	8	9	10	11	12	13	14	15	16	17	18	19	20	21	22	23	24	25	26	27	28	29	30	31

May

Cat of the Nile, 1987

monday
14 134

Sandy 10:00

Maggy

tuesday
15 135

Pat Wilson

wednesday
16 136

Vicki Haufuss - 10:00 - 832-8507

Pam   - 3:00 - 804-0093

                  ME - 4:30 - WITH DAVE COWON

Frod & Gloria Schindel

thursday
17 137
(4

Brian Haraga 2:30

(Chilliwack) Jan   4:00

friday
18 138
8.5

ARMED FORCES DAY

saturday
19 139
8.5

Lynx
The truly wise person
kneels at the feet of all creatures
and is not afraid to endure
the mockery of others.
    —Mechtild of Magdeburg

sunday
20 140

T	W	T	F	S	S	M	T	W	T	F	S	S	M	T	W	T	F	S	S	M	T	W	T	F	S	S	M	T	W	T
1	2	3	4	5	6	7	8	9	10	11	12	13	14	15	16	17	18	19	20	21	22	23	24	25	26	27	28	29	30	31

May

MAY

monday 21

Frod & Gloria

tuesday 22

7

10:00 Sandy

wednesday 23 ●

thursday 24

4

3:00 Toahvo Simmonson   1/2 hr

friday 25

6.5

4:00 Dave Cowon   1/2 hr

Pam 10:00

Gail Kurta 2:30 pm   832-0425

saturday 26

7

Linda,   10:00
(Vernon)

sunday 27

notes

monday
28 148

MEMORIAL DAY OBSERVED
BANK HOLIDAY (U.K.)

832-0997   GERI DAVY   1:30 PM
832-0425   GAIL KURTA   2:30 PM

tuesday
D **29** 149

8.5

wednesday
30 150

MEMORIAL DAY

8.5

GLORIA   5:30 PM   AT STORE

thursday
31 151
4

PAM MEYERS   10:00   **friday**
CONNIE JAMIESON   11:00   **1** 152
FRED SCHINDEL   12:00
LINDA   1:30 PM
GAIL KURTA   2:30 PM

DYLLON - REFLEXOLOGY   **saturday**
2 153

Raven Wolf

sunday
3 154

F	S	S	M	T	W	T	F	S	S	M	T	W	T	F	S	S	M	T	W	T	F	S	S	M	T	W	T	F	S
1	2	3	4	5	6	7	8	9	10	11	12	13	14	15	16	17	18	19	20	21	22	23	24	25	26	27	28	29	30

June

Raven Makes Magic

HINTON ALBERTA.

monday 4 155

ROSEMARIE CORNELL
DAVE MARQUIS
GINNETTE
DOUG BLOCHA
ELAINE PENNER
JOAN
MERVE

tuesday 5 156

ANITA HELLUM
LINDA REMPLE
GERRY EDWARDS
TAMMY MAYERS
TROY
BRIANNA
MICHEAL   AUSTIN (TROY'S SON)

wednesday 6 157

BEV BLOCHA
DONNA KENNEDY (BEV'S MOM)
PARISE   MICKEY (WITH DEBBIE)
ERIC MCNEIL
AMBER
FAY MCCRACKEN   ELI LASONDER - JIM TAYLOR

thursday 7 158

friday 8 159

Raven

Spirits

I can see

PAM MEYERS

They will come to me

They will come down under a cloud

They will be my masters

saturday 9 160

GLORIA SCHINDELL

I can see

They will walk in Raven town

   —Tlingit Vision Song

sunday 10 161

F	S	S	M	T	W	T	F	S	S	M	T	W	T	F	S	S	M	T	W	T	F	S	S	M	T	W	T	F	S
1	2	3	4	5	6	7	8	9	10	11	12	13	14	15	16	17	18	19	20	21	22	23	24	25	26	27	28	29	30

June

JUNE

monday
162 **11**   CONNIE JAMIESON   10:00

tuesday
163 **12**

wednesday
164 **13**
    3:30 ADREANNA (MOM AVA) 835-4790

thursday
165 **14**   STONEY PLAIN ALBERTA   FLAG DAY
                           PHASE V & VI COURSE

friday
166 **15**

saturday
167 **16**

sunday
168 **17**   FATHER'S DAY   notes

monday
18   169

RETURN HOME TODAY

tuesday
19   170

wednesday
20   171

SUMMER SOLSTICE 7:38 A.M. (GMT)

thursday
● 21   172

Untitled, 1978

friday
22   173

saturday
23   174

LINDA   10:00 (VERNON)

BRIANNA HARTLEY 11:00 (MOM DIANNA)

832-2663

sunday
24   175

F S S M T W T F S S M T W T F S S M T W T F S S M T W T F S
1 2 3 4 5 6 7 8 9 10 11 12 13 14 15 16 17 18 19 20 21 22 23 24 25 26 27 28 29 30

June

Bird Caller, 1976

monday
29   176

tuesday
26   177

wednesday
27   178

AWAY WITH
MARC

thursday
☽ 28   179

friday
29   180

saturday
30   181

Avian Spirits

Would that I were under the cliffs, in the secret hiding-places of the rocks, that Zeus might change me to a winged bird.

—Euripides, *Hippolytus*, l. 732

CANADA DAY (CANADA)

sunday
1   182

S	M	T	W	T	F	S	S	M	T	W	T	F	S	S	M	T	W	T	F	S	S	M	T	W	T	F	S	S	M	T
1	2	3	4	5	6	7	8	9	10	11	12	13	14	15	16	17	18	19	20	21	22	23	24	25	26	27	28	29	30	31

July

Kingfisher Dreams

monday 2 183

CANADA DAY OBSERVED (CANADA)

KELSEY 1:00 832-2228
$15.00 (MOM KAREN) KGNIA

tuesday 3 184

wednesday 4 185

INDEPENDENCE DAY

thursday 5 186

BILL STOVENSON 1:30 804-0264
GAIL KURTA 2:30 832-0425

PAM MEYERS 4:30

friday 6 187

DEBBIE GEDDES
832-8748

saturday 7 188

Kingfisher

All they could see was sky, water, birds,
light, and confluence. It was the whole
morning world.
—Eudora Welty,
The Optimist's Daughter

sunday 8 189

S	M	T	W	T	F	S	S	M	T	W	T	F	S	S	M	T	W	T	F	S	S	M	T	W	T	F	S	S	M	T
1	2	3	4	5	6	7	8	9	10	11	12	13	14	15	16	17	18	19	20	21	22	23	24	25	26	27	28	29	30	31

July

JULY

monday
9
190

JASON BRISBOS
ANNIBELLE
CLOEI
DEBBIE HOIT
ELI
SAMMUEL
KEVEN WILSON

tuesday
10
191

GARY LOVEGREEN
BRUCE WIGHTON
MERV MOUSER

wednesday
11
192

ROY MORROW
AUDREY GILBERT — CALL WHEN COMING BACK
MIKE GILBERT
FAY

thursday
12
193

BANK HOLIDAY (N. IRELAND)

MICKEY MULDAUN
ROCKY NOTNES

friday
13
194

HORM STEINGRUBE
GLORIA CALLIHOO

saturday
14
195

sunday
15
196

notes

monday
16 197

GLORIA SCHINDELL 1:30
KELSEY NGAI 2:00
SUSAN MUSSEL 3:00
SUE BOFIN 4:30

tuesday
17 198

wednesday
18 199

thursday
19 200

GAIL KURTIA 2:30
832-0425

friday
● 20 201

saturday
21 202

sunday
22 203

Untitled, 1979

S M T W T F S S M T W T F S S M T W T F S S M T W T F S S M T
1 2 3 4 5 6 7 8 9 10 11 12 13 14 15 16 17 18 19 20 21 22 23 24 25 26 27 28 29 30 31
July

Untitled, 1975

monday
23 204

tuesday
24 205

wednesday
25 206

Coyote

animal spirits
come round me
draw near me now
stand

thursday
26 207

listen you
invisible one
my scream's a storm
covering this world
leave this man
this sick one here
leave this man alone

friday
27 208

saturday
28 209

LINDA   10:00 AM

your invisible place
calls you calls you
go
    —from a Yukaghir (Siberian)
incantation to exorcise a demon

sunday
29 210

S M T W T F S S M T W T F S S M T W T F S S M T W T F S S M T
1 2 3 4 5 6 7 8 9 10 11 12 13 14 15 16 17 18 19 20 21 22 23 24 25 26 27 28 29 30 31

July

monday
211 30

tuesday
212 31

wednesday
213 1

thursday
214 2

friday
215 3

saturday
216 4 ○

sunday
217 5

notes

monday
6 218

BANK HOLIDAY (SCOTLAND)

tuesday
7 219

wednesday
8 220

DAVE COWEN 804-0802 thursday
AVA's DAUGHTER 11:00 AM **9** 221
835-4790

PAM MEYERS 804-0093
4:00 PM friday
10 222

saturday
11 223

sunday
12 224

Untitled, 1977

W T F S S M T W T F S S M T W T F S S M T W T F S S M T W T F
1 2 3 4 5 6 7 8 9 10 11 12 13 14 15 16 17 18 19 20 21 22 23 24 25 26 27 28 29 30 31
August

Arctic Tale, 1994

monday
13   225

tuesday
14   226

CONNIE JAMISON
ED HOUSS
548-3220

wednesday
15   227

thursday
16   228

Bear

A long way to go
a long way to climb
a long way to go to the sky

friday
17   229

Grizzly bear
rising
high behind the clouds

saturday
18   230

Paw tracks
make a circle
in the sky
—from a Tsimshian (Northwest Coast)
        trance song of a shaman

sunday
● 19   231

W T F S S M T W T F S S M T W T F S S M T W T F S S M T W T F
1 2 3 4 5 6 7 8 9 10 11 12 13 14 15 16 17 18 19 20 21 22 23 24 25 26 27 28 29 30 31
August

monday
232 **20**

tuesday
233 **21**

wednesday
234 **22**

thursday
235 **23**

HINTON ALBERTA

ROCKY

MARY SHARP   865-7695   WK 865-2211
CARMIN SMITH   865-7695
ROB LABBE   (BEU'S SON)
BARB KNOTOFF   ANNIBELLS & CLOE'

friday
236 **24**

MARY CORMO
DOUG BLOACA
ELI & PARISE
ROB ROACH
DORIS

saturday
237 **25** ☽

sunday   notes
238 **26**

monday
27 239

BANK HOLIDAY (U.K. EXCEPT SCOTLAND)

ROCKY
JOHN
BRIAN LALONDE
MARIA
LEILA

tuesday
28 240

PHONE WHEN COMING BACK → MARIO
MARY SHARP.

wednesday
29 241

thursday
30 242

friday
31 243

Untitled, 1986

saturday
1 244

sunday
2 245

S S M T W T F S S M T W T F S S M T W T F S S M T W T F S S
1 2 3 4 5 6 7 8 9 10 11 12 13 14 15 16 17 18 19 20 21 22 23 24 25 26 27 28 29 30
September

Untitled, 1974

monday
3
246

LABOR DAY (U.S. AND CANADA)

tuesday
4
247

ED House - 548-3220

wednesday
5
248

thursday
6
249

friday
7
250

Susan Musil

Forest Sprite

Upon a
little cloud
I ascend;
thus I journey upward
to a holy place
I go,
changing as I
pass through the air.

—Apache medicine song

saturday
8
251

sunday
9
252

S	S	M	T	W	T	F	S	S	M	T	W	T	F	S	S	M	T	W	T	F	S	S	M	T	W	T	F	S	S
1	2	3	4	5	6	7	8	9	10	11	12	13	14	15	16	17	18	19	20	21	22	23	24	25	26	27	28	29	30

September

SEPTEMBER

monday
253 **10**

tuesday
254 **11**

JULIE VANMALE   3:30 PM   -(GIFT CERTIFICATE)
HM 804-6365   WK 832-1334

wednesday
255 **12**

thursday
256 **13**

friday
257 **14**

saturday
258 **15**

sunday
259 **16**   *notes*

monday
● **17** 260

ROSH HASHANAH (BEGINS AT SUNSET)

tuesday
18 261

wednesday
19 262

VERA

thursday
20 263

ED HOUSS 12:00
ANNS BRIGGS 1:00

friday
21 264

SUSAN MUSIC

saturday
22 265

AUTUMNAL EQUINOX 11:04 P.M. (GMT)

sunday
23 266

Untitled, 1979

S	S	M	T	W	T	F	S	S	M	T	W	T	F	S	S	M	T	W	T	F	S	S	M	T	W	T	F	S	S
1	2	3	4	5	6	7	8	9	10	11	12	13	14	15	16	17	18	19	20	21	22	23	24	25	26	27	28	29	30

September

Griffin, 1975

HINTON

ROCKY
CRYSTA BROWN
CRYSTAL
ANDREW

GORDIE M^cCRACKEN
MICHEAL
GINNETTE

YOM KIPPUR (BEGINS AT SUNSET)

LEWI
MARIO
HARRY

MICHEAL
BIANCA HANNULA
ELI
SWEAT

VERNA ANDERSON

Griffin

In the very earliest times, when both people and animals lived on earth, a person could become an animal if he wanted to and an animal could become a human being. Sometimes they were people and sometimes animals, and there was no difference. All spoke the same language. That was the time when words were like magic.

—Netsilik Eskimo

S S M T W T F S S M T W T F S S M T W T F S S M T W T F S S
1 2 3 4 5 6 7 8 9 10 11 12 13 14 15 16 17 18 19 20 21 22 23 24 25 26 27 28 29 30

September

Jaguar Legend

monday
1
274

tuesday
2
275

wednesday
3
276

thursday
4
277

CONNIE JAMISON   10:00 AM
BACK REMODIGS - ED HOUSS   3:00 PM
SUE McPHARLEW   11:00 AM
675-4799

friday
5
278

Panther

Grandmother Earth, hear me! . . . The
two-leggeds, the four-leggeds, the
wingeds, and all that move upon You
are Your children. With all beings and
all things we shall be as relatives; just as
we are related to You, O Mother, so we
shall make peace with another people
and shall be related to them.

—Black Elk

saturday
6
279

sunday
7
280

M	T	W	T	F	S	S	M	T	W	T	F	S	S	M	T	W	T	F	S	S	M	T	W	T	F	S	S	M	T	W
1	2	3	4	5	6	7	8	9	10	11	12	13	14	15	16	17	18	19	20	21	22	23	24	25	26	27	28	29	30	31

October

OCTOBER

monday
281 **8**

COLUMBUS DAY OBSERVED
THANKSGIVING DAY (CANADA)

tuesday
282 **9**

wednesday
283 **10**

thursday
284 **11**

friday
285 **12**

COLUMBUS DAY

saturday
286 **13**

sunday
287 **14**

notes

monday
15 288

tuesday
• 16 289

wednesday
17 290

thursday
18 291

ED HOUSE   12:00 PM

KIMBERLEY   4:00 PM (PREGNANT.)
(HUSBAND LANCE)   838-0158

friday
19 292

saturday
20 293

Night Form, 1973

sunday
21 294

M T W T F S S M T W T F S S M T W T F S S M T W T F S S M T W T F S S M T W
1 2 3 4 5 6 7 8 9 10 11 12 13 14 15 16 17 18 19 20 21 22 23 24 25 26 27 28 29 30 31
October

Untitled, 1975

monday
22 295

tuesday
23 296

ROCKY
CATHY MARTIN
AUDREY GILBERT
PAUL PELLEY
JENALLE BEVERLY

UNITED NATIONS DAY

wednesday
D 24 297

TROY
MARIO
ELI
SAMUEL

thursday
25 298

SANDRA PELLEY
RITA WILLIAMS
COLLEN (TROY'S MOM)
JORDON PELLEY
JACI   "

MICHEAL

friday
26 299

DEBBIE
CATHEREN DUFFEY
COLLEREN BURKHERT
MATT
KELSEY

saturday
27 300

Doe

On the trail marked with pollen may I walk,

With grasshoppers about my feet may I walk,

With dew about my feet may I walk,

With beauty may I walk. . . .

—Navajo

DAYLIGHT SAVING TIME ENDS

sunday
28 301

M	T	W	T	F	S	S	M	T	W	T	F	S	S	M	T	W	T	F	S	S	M	T	W	T	F	S	S	M	T	W
1	2	3	4	5	6	7	8	9	10	11	12	13	14	15	16	17	18	19	20	21	22	23	24	25	26	27	28	29	30	31

October

monday
29
302

tuesday
30
303

wednesday
31
304

HALLOWEEN

thursday
1 ○
305

friday
2
306

saturday
3
307

sunday
4
308

notes

monday
5 309

tuesday
6 310

ELECTION DAY

wednesday
7 311
AT HM

LOUISA GOLBRANBI'S WAYSON 10:00
SON →

thursday
8 312

PAM MAYORS 10:00

friday
9 313

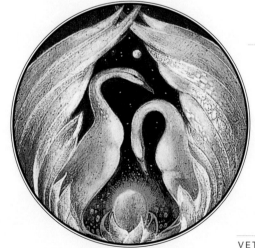

saturday
10 314

Untitled, 1980

VETERANS DAY
REMEMBRANCE DAY (CANADA)

sunday
11 315

T F S S M T W T F S S M T W T F S S M T W T F S S M T W T F
1 2 3 4 5 6 7 8 9 10 11 12 13 14 15 16 17 18 19 20 21 22 23 24 25 26 27 28 29 30
November

Untitled, 1979

monday
12   316

VETERANS DAY OBSERVED
REMEMBRANCE DAY OBSERVED (CANADA)

tuesday
13   317

wednesday
14   318

thursday
● 15   319

Ram

Only to the white man was nature a "wilderness," and only to him was the land "infested" with "wild" animals and "savage" people. To us it was tame. Earth was bountiful, and we were surrounded with the blessings of the Great Mystery. Not until the hairy man from the east came . . . was it "wild" for us. When the very animals of the forest began fleeing from his approach, then it was that for us the "Wild West" began.
— Luther Standing Bear,
Land of the Spotted Eagle

friday
16   320

SUSAN MUSIC

saturday
17   321

sunday
18   322

T F S S M T W T F S S M T W T F S S M T W T F S S M T W T F
1 2 3 4 5 6 7 8 9 10 11 12 13 14 15 16 17 18 19 20 21 22 23 24 25 26 27 28 29 30
November

NOVEMBER

monday
323 **19**

tuesday
324 **20**

wednesday
325 **21**

thursday
326 **22** ☽
THANKSGIVING DAY

friday
327 **23**

saturday
328 **24**

sunday
329 **25**
notes

monday
26
330

tuesday
27
331

wednesday
28
332

thursday
29
333

SUSAN MUSIC
DARLENE FOLK

friday
○ 30
334

saturday
1
335

Bear Totem

sunday
2
336

S S M T W T F S S M T W T F S S M T W T F S S M T W T F S S M T W T F S S M
1 2 3 4 5 6 7 8 9 10 11 12 13 14 15 16 17 18 19 20 21 22 23 24 25 26 27 28 29 30 31
December

Grandfather Wolf

monday
3 337

tuesday
4 338

wednesday
5 339

thursday
6 340

Wolf

A wolf
I considered myself
but I have eaten nothing
therefore from standing
I am tired out.

A wolf
I considered myself
but the owls are hooting
and the night
I fear.

—Teton Sioux

DARLENE FOLK

friday
7 341

saturday
8 342

FIRST NIGHT OF HANUKKAH

sunday
9 343

S	S	M	T	W	T	F	S	S	M	T	W	T	F	S	S	M	T	W	T	F	S	S	M	T	W	T	F	S	S	M
1	2	3	4	5	6	7	8	9	10	11	12	13	14	15	16	17	18	19	20	21	22	23	24	25	26	27	28	29	30	31

December

DECEMBER

monday
344 **10**

tuesday
345 **11**

wednesday
346 **12**

thursday
347 **13**

friday
348 **14** ● SUSAN MUSIC
DARLENE FOCK

saturday
349 **15**

sunday
350 **16**

notes

monday
17 351

tuesday
18 352

wednesday
19 353

thursday
20 354

WINTER SOLSTICE 7:21 P.M. (GMT)

friday
21 355

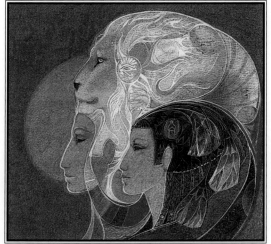

saturday
D 22 356

Untitled, 1976

sunday
23 357

S S M T W T F S S M T W T F S S M T W T F S S M T W T F S S M
1 2 3 4 5 6 7 8 9 10 11 12 13 14 15 16 17 18 19 20 21 22 23 24 25 26 27 28 29 30 31
December

Totem, 1983

monday
24
358

DARLENE

tuesday
25
359

CHRISTMAS DAY

wednesday
26
360

KWANZAA BEGINS
BOXING DAY (CANADA, U.K.)

thursday
27
361

friday
28
362

Eagle
Screaming the night away
With his great wing feathers
Swooping the darkness up;
I hear the Eagle bird
Pulling the blanket back
Off from the eastern sky.

—Iroquois

saturday
29
363

sunday
30
364

S S M T W T F S S M T W T F S S M T W T F S S M T W T F S S M
1 2 3 4 5 6 7 8 9 10 11 12 13 14 15 16 17 18 19 20 21 22 23 24 25 26 27 28 29 30 31

December

monday
365
31

MAGGIE PYM (AT HM)
832-4515

tuesday
1
1

NEW YEAR'S DAY

wednesday
2
2

BANK HOLIDAY (SCOTLAND)

thursday
3
3

friday
4
4

saturday
5
5

sunday
6
6

notes

Untitled, 1973

2001 •

January

S	M	T	W	T	F	S
	1	2	3	4	5	6
7	8	9	10	11	12	13
14	15	16	17	18	19	20
21	22	23	24	25	26	27
28	29	30	31			

May

S	M	T	W	T	F	S
		1	2	3	4	5
6	7	8	9	10	11	12
13	14	15	16	17	18	19
20	21	22	23	24	25	26
27	28	29	30	31		

September

S	M	T	W	T	F	S
						1
2	3	4	5	6	7	8
9	10	11	12	13	14	15
16	17	18	19	20	21	22
23	24	25	26	27	28	29
30						

February

S	M	T	W	T	F	S
				1	2	3
4	5	6	7	8	9	10
11	12	13	14	15	16	17
18	19	20	21	22	23	24
25	26	27	28			

June

S	M	T	W	T	F	S
					1	2
3	4	5	6	7	8	9
10	11	12	13	14	15	16
17	18	19	20	21	22	23
24	25	26	27	28	29	30

October

S	M	T	W	T	F	S
	1	2	3	4	5	6
7	8	9	10	11	12	13
14	15	16	17	18	19	20
21	22	23	24	25	26	27
28	29	30	31			

March

S	M	T	W	T	F	S
				1	2	3
4	5	6	7	8	9	10
11	12	13	14	15	(16)	17
18	19	20	21	22	23	24
25	26	27	28	29	30	31

July

S	M	T	W	T	F	S
1	2	3	4	5	6	7
8	9	10	11	12	13	14
15	16	17	18	19	20	21
22	23	24	25	26	27	28
29	30	31				

November

S	M	T	W	T	F	S
				1	2	3
4	5	6	7	8	9	10
11	12	13	14	15	16	17
18	19	20	21	22	23	24
25	26	27	28	29	30	

April

S	M	T	W	T	F	S
1	2	3	4	5	6	7
8	9	10	11	12	13	14
15	16	17	18	19	20	21
22	23	24	25	26	27	28
29	30					

August

S	M	T	W	T	F	S
			1	2	3	4
5	6	7	8	9	10	11
12	13	14	15	16	17	18
19	20	21	22	23	24	25
26	27	28	29	30	31	

December

S	M	T	W	T	F	S
						1
2	3	4	5	6	7	8
9	10	11	12	13	14	15
16	17	18	19	20	21	22
23	24	25	26	27	28	29
30	31					

•2002

January

S	M	T	W	T	F	S
		1	2	3	4	5
6	7	8	9	10	11	12
13	14	15	16	17	18	19
20	21	22	23	24	25	26
27	28	29	30	31		

May

S	M	T	W	T	F	S
			1	2	3	4
5	6	7	8	9	10	11
12	13	14	15	16	17	18
19	20	21	22	23	24	25
26	27	28	29	30	31	

September

S	M	T	W	T	F	S
1	2	3	4	5	6	7
8	9	10	11	12	13	14
15	16	17	18	19	20	21
22	23	24	25	26	27	28
29	30					

February

S	M	T	W	T	F	S
					1	2
3	4	5	6	7	8	9
10	11	12	13	14	15	16
17	18	19	20	21	22	23
24	25	26	27	28		

June

S	M	T	W	T	F	S
						1
2	3	4	5	6	7	8
9	10	11	12	13	14	15
16	17	18	19	20	21	22
23	24	25	26	27	28	29
30						

October

S	M	T	W	T	F	S
		1	2	3	4	5
6	7	8	9	10	11	12
13	14	15	16	17	18	19
20	21	22	23	24	25	26
27	28	29	30	31		

March

S	M	T	W	T	F	S
					1	2
3	4	5	6	7	8	9
10	11	12	13	14	15	16
17	18	19	20	21	22	23
24	25	26	27	28	29	30
31						

July

S	M	T	W	T	F	S
	1	2	3	4	5	6
7	8	9	10	11	12	13
14	15	16	17	18	19	20
21	22	23	24	25	26	27
28	29	30	31			

November

S	M	T	W	T	F	S
					1	2
3	4	5	6	7	8	9
10	11	12	13	14	15	16
17	18	19	20	21	22	23
24	25	26	27	28	29	30

April

S	M	T	W	T	F	S
	1	2	3	4	5	6
7	8	9	10	11	12	13
14	15	16	17	18	19	20
21	22	23	24	25	26	27
28	29	30				

August

S	M	T	W	T	F	S
				1	2	3
4	5	6	7	8	9	10
11	12	13	14	15	16	17
18	19	20	21	22	23	24
25	26	27	28	29	30	31

December

S	M	T	W	T	F	S
1	2	3	4	5	6	7
8	9	10	11	12	13	14
15	16	17	18	19	20	21
22	23	24	25	26	27	28
29	30	31				

personal information.

name _____

address _____

city _____

state _____ zip _____

home phone _____ fax_____

work phone _____ cell/pager_____

email _____

in case of emergency, please notify:

name _____

address _____

city _____

state _____ zip _____

phone_____

medical information:

physician's name _____

physician's phone _____

health insurance company _____

plan number _____

allergies _____

other_____

other information:

driver's license number _____

car insurance company _____

policy number _____